Look…No Hands!

A moment of crisis at a bounce into water
turned out all right because of good training techniques.

It's not magic!
It's teaching the skills *correctly*
so that in a 'crisis moment'
the *correct* response happens.

Look...No Hands!
Straightforward Cross-Country

ERIC SMILEY FBHS

First published in the UK in 2009
by The Pony Club, Kenilworth, Warwickshire cv8 2rw

British Library Cataloguing-in-Publication Data
A catalogue record for this book
is available from the British Library

ISBN 978 0 9561071 1 4

Exercise diagrams by Rachael Tremlett, Rodney Paull, Micha Gomes and Oliver Tobey.
Other illustrations by Maggie Raynor.
Photographs by or courtesy of the author.

Printed in England by Halstan & Co. Ltd., Amersham

Distributed for The Pony Club by
Kenilworth Press
An imprint of Quiller Publishing Ltd
Wykey House, Wykey, Shrewsbury, sy4 1ja
Tel: 01939 261616 Fax: 01939 261606
E-mail: info@quillerbooks.com
Website: www.kenilworthpress.co.uk

Contents

Preface
Eric and the Pony Club

I became a member of the Killultagh, Old Rock and Chichester Harriers Pony Club at the age of eleven. We had just moved from Belfast to the country where my parents had bought a small farm. Both my parents were doctors in Belfast. My father was a consultant thoracic surgeon at the Royal Victoria Hospital but had come from a country background in Castlewellan, Co. Down. Whilst in Belfast he used to keep a horse with a wonderful man called Archie Willis. Moving to 'Streamville' in the parish of Magheragall was a move that would change the lives of our whole family.

My brothers, Chris and Ian joined the Killultagh branch of the Pony Club with me. A few years later Fiona, my younger sister was also to join.

It became quite a family interest as my father was keen to hunt and he introduced us all to the joys of crossing the country. In those days we had a car and single trailer so the logistics of getting us to the meet or the rally were interesting. We would start hacking in the direction of the PC rally and my father would drive one pony and child depositing them a few miles from the venue, he would then return to collect the next pony and rider. We had to know the route and have prearranged meeting places. Occasionally this didn't work, much to the annoyance of my long-suffering father. Eventually we would all arrive at the rally to have a great few hours instruction and fun. I believe this method of travel is called 'boxing and coxing'!

It introduced me, not only to the joys of the Pony Club but also to the pleasure to be had spending time in the saddle. One got to know one's pony and in doing so developed all sorts of instinctive skills. The grass verges were great places to trot, the small ditches were good to jump and we would always find someone's field where we could have a canter.

The hunting kindled my interest in cross-country: the excitement of the unexpected and the thrill of jumping the same hedges and ditches that the horses were jumping. All this from the back of a 12.2hh pony never really seemed daunting.

Our branch of the Pony Club was fairly competitive although not that large in numbers. We were always 'game' and ready to 'have a go' and what we lacked in finesse we made up for in the ability to gallop and jump. This gave me a feel for getting on and doing, often without any idea of how and why. I have no recollection of anyone filling in these blanks in my education until much later in my riding career.

As time went on, my brothers developed other interests and I remained the one smitten. I show jumped and evented through the summer and hunted with my father in the winter. I was mounted on an interesting collection of ponies and small horses, some more successful than others. My love for greys started with a pony called 'Silverstream', a 13.2hh flea-bitten grey mare, a very Thoroughbred type. She was great at the walk and trot race, impatient in the sack race, very fast in the show jumping and just brilliant cross-country.

'Ginger' my first 14.2hh used to buck me off so I learned about falling, trying to stay on and how to avoid injury. Skills which were invaluable to learn.

I progressed through the Pony Club, gaining my B test ... just, and then joined the Army. I was able to ride throughout my time in the Army, playing polo, hunting, team chasing, eventing and show jumping. My next great learning experience was at the Royal Army Veterinary Corps depot at Melton Mowbray. Here the chief instructor, Captain Ben Jones, was an inspiration. Formerly Sergeant Ben Jones and a prominent member of the British team on such horses as The Poacher. He opened my eyes to refining new skills. He was a natural horseman but unlike many others he was also able to explain and demonstrate the hows and whys I had missed in my earlier riding. My time spent with him, although only six weeks, was to be the catalyst for the decision about my future career.

On leaving the Army I spent nine months at Talland School of Equitation under the expert tuition of Mrs Molly Sivewright, ably assisted by Pammy Hutton and John Mansfield. This time was invaluable as it gave

above I never did grow into the breeches

above right At home – ready to go

right Spot the enthusiast

11

me inspired teaching on lovely horses, an insight into riding at a much higher level and an instinct of how to make things happen.

The Pony Club was the start, Ben Jones was the inspiration, and Talland was the structure … I had become driven.

I left Talland with my British Horse Society's Instructor certificate and returned to Ireland to run an eventing centre. Within five years I had produced a horse from novice to 4 star and was selected to represent Ireland at the European Championships. In the following twenty years I passed my British Horse Society Fellowship exam and have competed at European, World and Olympic level. I have enjoyed producing many horses to Advanced level and travelling the world teaching.

The Pony Club was the start …

Introduction
What the Book is About

Riding across the country, whether it be hunting, eventing, hunter trials or just being out in the country is one of the most exhilarating experiences we can have with our pony or horse. There is always the sense of the excitement of the unexpected, the bigger than normal fence, the uncertainty of direction or line to be taken. To make the most of this experience it is important to understand what makes it all such fun, and for both horse/pony and rider to be prepared. As instructors and coaches we play a vital role in guiding the human and equine partnership to enjoy this experience as safely as is possible. It's about managing the risk.

Totally safe cross-country riding isn't possible. It is more an understanding of the process: a progressive training method that links flat work and jumping with the appropriate division of responsibilities for rider and horse. This publication will clarify these responsibilities.

Acknowledgements

Immense thanks to my wife Sue for all her hard work and encouragement.

Thanks also to Susan Irwin and Hannah Dunbar.

1

Start Point

It is important to understand the requirements of a riding horse. It must be fun and easy to ride. This is the same for a hack as it is for a Grand Prix dressage horse or a hunter. A pleasant ride is a horse that does what is asked of him and performs willingly. This is only possible with an acceptance of a partnership.

- The rider to ride and ask …

- the horse to be asked and to do.

It is important to retain this understanding of a partnership.

'Do what I say' is hardly a partnership.

'Joint decisions' sometimes take discussion time.

The rider must retain the overall responsibility to guide and direct, being the only one who knows what the partnership is going to do and how it is to be done. To understand partnerships and how they work is an important part of training for the instructor and rider.

Certain guidelines, rules and boundaries must exist in order to create a framework within which to work. These boundaries must be created with an understanding of where the horse is coming from and what is his natural existence. As a herd animal he is subject to rules imposed by the herd and its hierarchy. These rules are enforced and adhered to by the herd otherwise anarchy takes over.

To simulate these rules, when the rider becomes the herd leader, consistency and clarity are important, as we are then more easily understood and accepted by the horse. Boundaries must be clear and although they may be challenged they must be consistent. Enforcement of these boundaries **does not** mean physical punishment.

Sometimes a look or a movement from a fellow herd member is enough to make the point. The character of the individual receiving the warning is important to know. Some horses/ponies and riders need very little to make the point very clear.

Establishing these boundaries and codes of conduct takes time and experimentation. Sometimes mistakes are made on both sides. The rider and trainer will both need to feel their way into the establishment of boundaries.

- Too severe and speedy implementation may cause rebellion

- too lax and unclear instructions may lead to misunderstanding and uncertainty.

C is for Clear. The message from trainer to pupil and pupil to horse must be clear, using words or descriptions that can be understood at the level of the recipient.

F is for Fair. 'Is the message fair?' means does the pupil understand what is being asked for and what they need to do and how to do it. In turn, does the horse know or understand what is being asked of him. Is the message compatible with its level of fitness, its age and education, its timing in the session?

C is now for Consistent. Is the message consistent, the same as every other time? To encourage a consistent response the message must be consistent. The rider must have sufficient understanding of how and what to apply and be in good enough balance so that the message can be applied the same way each time. It is illogical to expect the horse or rider to be mind-readers and guess what is required.

These three words can be used to question: is it Clear, Fair or Consistent? If not, then it becomes the challenge to rephrase the input to make it clearer to horse and rider. The clearer and more consistent we are in communication with pupil and horse the more likely we are to produce a happy and productive partnership.

Clear, Fair and Consistent

2

How Learning Happens

Much of the start point will have been established when 'starting' the young horse.

The riding horse's start point must be the acceptance of the rider. To start with the acceptance of his presence and then the understanding of the means of communication. Known as 'the Aids', these means of communication must be kept C. F. C. and very simple.

As humans we tend to try and liken a horse's intelligence with that of our own. We assume much and are often disappointed when expectations are not realised. The intelligence of a horse is very different from that of a human. Our ability to reason and think a subject through to its logical conclusion is not often mirrored by that of the horse. Their highly complex instinctive reactions and interaction requires understanding, if we are to 'marry the minds' to form a working relationship. One that relies on trust, respect and an understanding of responsibilities. To achieve this the expression 'know your horse' is important on many levels. Know the species, its origins and history. Understand its lifestyle as a herd animal. Appreciate how we have changed it over the generations of selective breeding. Try to think what it is thinking as we endeavour to communicate our will and desire for it to do what we want. A failure to do this produces a relationship built on dictatorship. History shows that true potential can never be realised when the character of the individual is suppressed.

Horses learn mainly through 'conditioned reflex'. Repeating a process many times through a certain set of stimuli produces a certain response. Repeat the stimuli and the action becomes a habit.

Horses do not reason that legs on, means go forward or that left rein means go left. If, however, the stimuli is followed by the correct action and a reward is given they begin to feel good about the response, then this becomes a habit: Positive Response.

If the incorrect action occurs, the horse must be made aware that this is not what was asked for by the rider. It may go through a number of responses before a reward is given to acknowledge the correct response; this will trigger the correct answer to the stimuli.

The more often the sequence of correct responses occurs the more the correct habit will be enforced.

Good practice is where we Practise Perfect or as near as we can and this becomes Perfect Practice which is reinforcing the good habit.

As instructors we need to understand how learning takes place and how we can facilitate this learning.

Mr Conscious

I'm Mr Conscious, I'm part of the brain that thinks, reasons and makes considered decisions. I instruct my body to act, when asked to do so. I teach Mr Subconscious what to do. He is rather a methodical person

who acts on instructions. However, he does take over some of the more mundane habitual tasks. Providing I teach him the correct way we have a good working relationship.

Mr Subconscious

I'm Mr Subconscious. I'm part of the brain that looks after everything termed as 'habits'. When Mr Conscious is thinking, I'm doing. He may teach me what to do but once I have learned the skill I need no further help. I am dependable and consistent with my responses and will only do what I have been conditioned to do. I do not change my ways easily – some would say I'm stubborn, I require a good reason and plenty of practice in order to change. Mr Conscious and I get on well together.

Mr Coach

I'm Mr Coach. My job is to work closely with Mr Conscious and Mr Subconscious. Mr Conscious would normally listen, think and is able to reason what I am trying to teach him. Once he understands that, he is normally fairly straightforward to work with. This thought process does, however, take a little time which can slow down the 'action' and 'reaction' time. Mr Subconscious is not so easy initially. He requires his lessons to be very clear and to be repeated often. He does not understand right from wrong but just does what Mr Conscious and I teach him. Care is therefore important. Once he gets the message, he is great, because we seldom have to repeat the lesson and unprompted he just keeps producing the right answer.

Mr Horse

I'm Mr Horse, I, too have a conscious and a subconscious, however my ability to reason and have intelligent thought is limited. I eat grass for a living! My subconscious is well developed and I am most eager to please and very dependable if taught well.

The Senses

As instructors we can facilitate the learning experience by using as many of the senses as possible. We must be aware that each pupil and horse learns in a slightly different way, at different speeds and with different priorities.

We need to prioritise what is important at any given time and in doing so may have to accept that other tasks may not be taken in at that time. As part of progressive training we can always return to the subject and fill in the gaps. The more reinforcement of seeing, doing and feeling something happening right, the more pupils begin to perform the task without thinking.

As instructors we need to break down tasks into manageable sizes and then piece them together again into the whole.

The logic and clarity of Mr Conscious must be very clear and well practised by Mr Subconscious before he takes over and the lesson is learnt and secure.

3

The Aids, Qualities and Language

We are all individuals and as such have our own way of explaining ourselves. Heaven forbid this ever stops, as it makes for a colourful existence with characters and creative instructors. We do, however, have a responsibility to know the language we use and to use it correctly. To do so must surely make our pupils understanding, both human and equine, clearer.

When we talk, teach and ride qualities that mean the same to everyone it is much easier to be specific about what is good and what is not good. It becomes easier for pupils to understand what they need to do, and to retain the good and correct the not so good.

Let's Start with the Aids

The leg aids

There are two sets of leg aids. On the girth are forward riding aids. Behind the girth are sideways moving aids. Both legs on the girth means go forward. One leg behind the girth means go sideways as well as forward.

The rein aids

Both reins control the speed. The inside rein is also responsible for direction whilst the outside rein creates a boundary for the outside of the horse.

Much is talked about how these aids are used. As things happen quickly when going cross-country, I believe it is important that these aids are **simple and clear. No discussion, no misunderstanding, no doubt what the response is to be.**

Qualities

The acceptance of the 'Scales of Training' worldwide is understood. It provides the framework for a sound education of the horse from the beginning to the highest level. Some of the words used in teaching need to have a snappy explanation to enable riders to take on board the meaning quickly, for example:

Forward – them taking us

Straight – quarters following – forehand – following – head on any given line the rider chooses

Rhythm – footfall of the gait

Regularity – ability to maintain a gait

Balance – even distribution of weight

Acceptance and understanding – acceptance without understanding isn't enough

As instructors we must encourage the riders to live these words and qualities.

Think them, teach them and ride them.

Language

Let me clarify some misunderstandings of popular expressions:

Between leg and hand. Never the other way as the leg is the primary aid and should always be used, talked about and thought of first.

Bend your horse around the inside leg. This has little to do with the inside leg as it merely acts as a 'post' for every other aid to bend the horse around.

Half halt. Both legs to both hands, *not* fiddling with the out side rein.

More leg. The law of diminishing returns says 'the more you use the less you get'. This should mean get more from the leg you are using, not more leg.

Inside leg to outside hand. When ridden between both legs to an accepting contact, the horse will appear to be on the outside rein or hand, because the inside rein guides and is light. There is no need to drive the horse outwards.

The picture below illustrates **on the bit and between the aids**.

The sequence is:

Legs ➤ Quarters ➤ Back ➤ Poll ➤ Jaw ➤ Bit ➤ Hand

All must be accepted and understood for a horse to be on the bit and between the aids.

Rhythm. Often misused to cover many qualities, all at the same time. It is the footfall of the gait. Rhythm is either correct or it isn't.

Regularity. This is the ability to maintain the consistency of a gait or pace.

Don't confuse them! For example, a four-time canter can be very *regular* but the *rhythm* is incorrect.

Tempo. This is the speed of the rhythm. Often misused as a word, but it should be thought of as improving the *quality* of the gait or pace.

Instructor. The teacher, trainer who teaches the skills of riding.

Coach. The person able to perform the Instructor's role, but also to guide and mentor the progress of the bigger picture.

C³

C is for **Contact**. Contact is what the rider has between his hand and the horse's mouth.

Much is said and written about what it should be. It is to many people … different. To many horses it is different. We are all beings with different sensitivities. The common ground is that a contact must be humane and understood by both parties. I use the analogy of boyfriend/girlfriend holding hands. I know it's a bit corny but who wants to be held in a vice grip or like a wet fish … no one. Therefore, a comfortable hold which remains alive yet still is the aim.

C is also for **Connection**. Connection is the back end of a horse connected to the front end. Sometimes called 'coming through'; without resistance. No restriction to the flow of information, so the horse responds to the leg aid and takes the rider positively forward to the contact.

C is also for **Consistency**. The ability to make things remain the same: an outline of a horse, the regularity of a canter, the stride between jumps etc.

Without the first two the third is not possible.

> **As you will see, the use of language in its most correct sense is important to the communication between instructor and pupil, and pupil and horse.**

4

Balance and Position

Balance is the foundation of a good **position**. It allows us to use our communication easily without the interference of grip, i.e. the independent seat.

Balance and position have many governing factors, not least the human's physical shape. We come in all shapes, sizes and physical conditions. Each one of us co-ordinates movement in a slightly different way, depending on how we have learnt or how we have been taught.

The idea is to create a position that finds its balance without having to be told how to do it.

The conscious mind is always more receptive to thoughts if it knows why it is being asked to receive information and that the information is sound and makes sense. It then passes that message to the subconscious mind to make it happen without conscious thought. This is called conditioned reflex. This reflex must be taught in a very simple way.

When standing we have our feet underneath. Why? Because they support and carry our weight. Bend the knees, ankles and hips but still focus on looking ahead, i.e. where you are going, and the feet remain underneath you.

Practise this on the ground. Ask riders to adopt three different positions, for dressage, show jumping and cross-country. In many ways you will be able to see how they will sit when on a horse by doing this exercise. This is because they have a preconceived idea of what they should be like. There may be a need to change some aspects of their positions before even getting on a horse.

Now you are developing **muscle memory**.

Dressage

Shoulder, hip, heel

Classically correct

At all times the weight remains on the foot

Show jumping

Knee, toe

Hip and heel

Cross-country

Knee, toe

Closing the angle at the ankle, knee and hip

Each time the instructor says or the rider hears 'heels down' beware. Often riders will react to something being said to others as a correction, by doing it themselves. They may not need to correct this issue but now they have forced their heel down unnecessarily.

The ball of the foot should be on the stirrup, the ankle flexible and the heel approximately 2cm/1inch lower than the ball of the foot.

Correct

27

Common faults:

- lower leg swinging back because weight is on ball of foot and ankle is not soft and relaxed

- lower leg is back because upper body is too far forward

- lower leg swinging forward because the heel is too low.

Heel too high in both the above photos

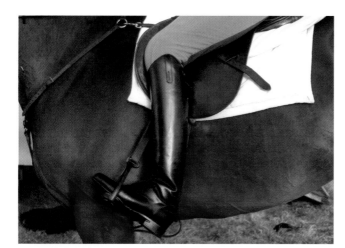

Heel too low

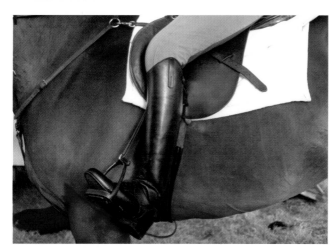

Heel too low

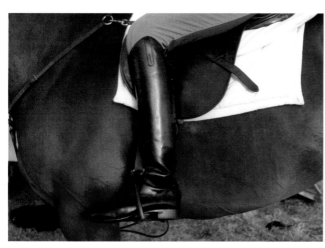

Toes down

Much is taught about leg position, but I find the easiest way is to give the leg a function or job to do, and it normally finds its own position, which happens to be the correct one. The most obvious function is to carry the rider's weight, therefore the foot must lie directly underneath the body weight.

Foot/Stirrup Relationship

Much depends on the physical shape of the rider and where they are comfortable in the saddle.

There are, however, some measures to help in the instruction of a good stirrup length. The following applies when the horse is standing still:

- If the knee is in the knee roll and the seat is in the seat of the saddle … you're riding too long!

- If the knee is in the knee roll the seat should be on the back of the saddle towards the cantle.

- If the seat is in the saddle, the knee should be on top of the knee roll.

This will allow the rider to 'fit' into the knee roll when they are in a light seat. The leg is then secure and the rider more able to remain in balance.

On the horse ask the rider to stand in the stirrups and find a position that is like standing on the ground and that is comfortable. Minor adjustments can be made to simulate the positions that they had when standing on the ground. Time spent doing this and encouraging riders to feel what muscles they must move to adjust their balance to stand comfortably is time well spent – **Muscle Memory**.

Now adjust the stirrups to jump length, maybe at this stage not as short as cross-country length. Find the balance again while standing in the stirrups. *See* photos on pages 27 or 31.

This is an important stage. The rider must feel no tension or difficulty in maintaining balance. They must adjust or move whatever part of the body is necessary to relieve the tension and find 'perfect balance'. A neck strap is sometimes helpful to assist the rider.

Now ask the rider to maintain the balance at the walk. First timers often find this easier than riders you are trying to correct.

Secure position

Give the rider simple tasks to undertake, such as turns, transitions and changes of direction. The rules are clear, the rider may not sit or look down. Each time the rider loses balance ask them where that loss of balance came from. Most of the time it will be that the heel has gone too low or too high. Identify the cause and encourage correction. Carry on with the simple riding exercises, giving the legs and reins a purpose, i.e. support of the rider and guidance of the horse.

Some horses become anxious and misunderstand the new leg position, mainly because the rider starts to grip for fear of losing their balance or because the leg has never been there before. In the first instance let the rider rest their hands against the horse's neck and relax the leg and in the second instance encourage the rider to keep the leg quietly against the horse's side as it becomes accustomed to its presence.

This exercise can also be done at trot and canter and eventually over a pole, progressing to a small jump whilst remaining in a light seat.

Riders now tend to feel they should fold from the hip as the horse goes over a small jump. Discourage an exaggerated movement. With a light seat in balance, the amount of movement should be small. Allow the horse to come up to you by being flexible through ankle, knee and hip as these joints absorb the jump.

To make a position and let it be sustainable and function correctly at all times requires the correct message process from brain to body.

This message must be put in place and practised for it to become second nature i.e. a habit that happens without thinking: **Muscle Memory**.

The correction of an existing message process is more difficult. It requires the removal of the existing, unwanted process, at the same time as one is trying to implant the new one. Be positive – think of what you want and why it is of benefit as this always speeds up the assimilation process.

5

School Exercises

Question: Why do we ride school exercises/movements?
Answer: To see if I can!

Question: So what if you can?
Answer: It means my horse is attentive to the Aids.

There is no magic in doing school exercises so to say that you do a circle or any other exercise to help improve the way the horse goes is illogical. It's not the circle that helps, it's the way you ride the line and the accuracy of the circle.

Relate the Three Phases

It is said that flat work is the foundation of all jumping. It's true, but why is it?

The skills of riding a dressage test are in part controlling a horse along a line at the required pace. The same can be said of show jumping and cross-country. The only difference is that now there are jumps along the line.

In relating the three phases I have highlighted some of the many common skills and qualities:

- control of line

- acceptance and understanding of the aid

- adjustment of speed up and down

- ability to turn both ways

- achieving balance.

So now put poles into the school movements.

There is an *endless* number of ways to use poles. I have chosen some to give an idea of their value. They are there to illustrate the importance of understanding the word **line**.

Trot Exercises

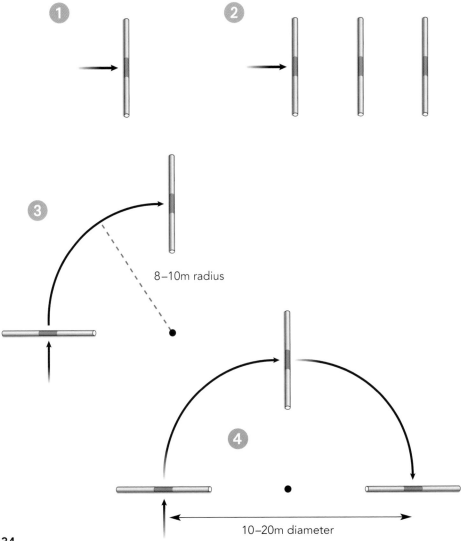

8–10m radius

10–20m diameter

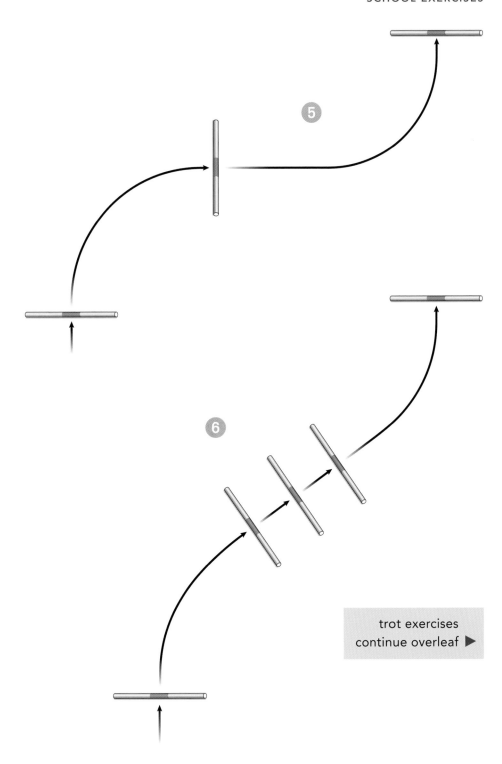

trot exercises
continue overleaf ▶

Wavy lines

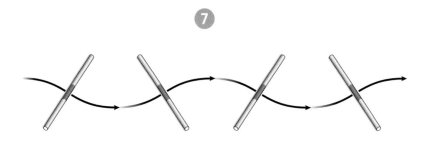

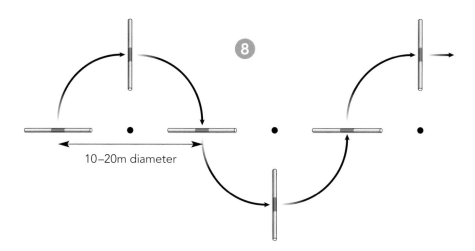

10–20m diameter

The distance between the poles is not critical as the line is the main challenge but in numbers 2 and 6 the three trotting poles should be between 1.20 and 1.50m apart.

Benefits

- challenges rider to be accurate

- improves co-ordination of Aid

- speeds a horse's reaction to Aid

- develops honesty to the Line

- develops competitive edge.

Canter Exercises

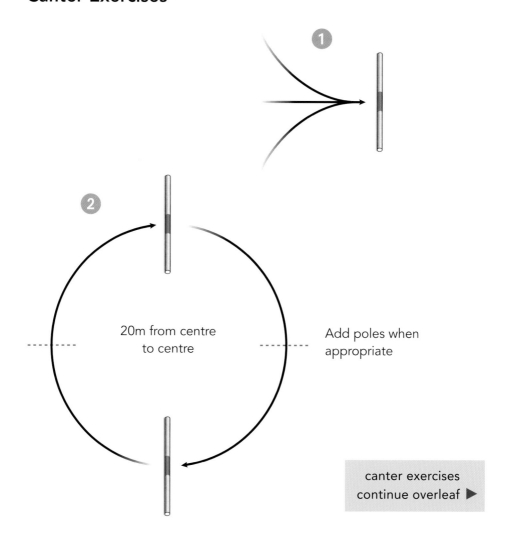

20m from centre
to centre

Add poles when
appropriate

canter exercises
continue overleaf ▶

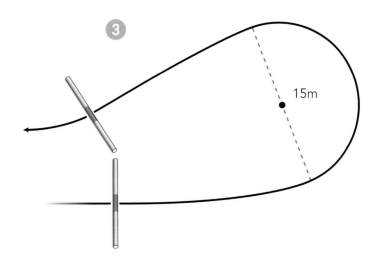

③

15m

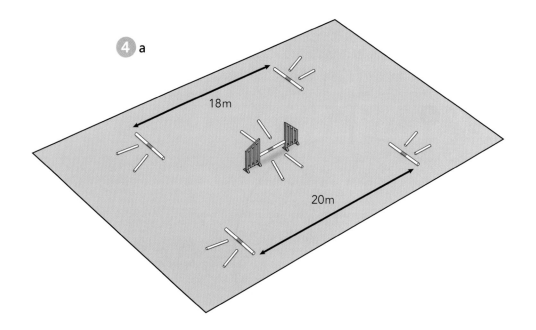

④ a

18m

20m

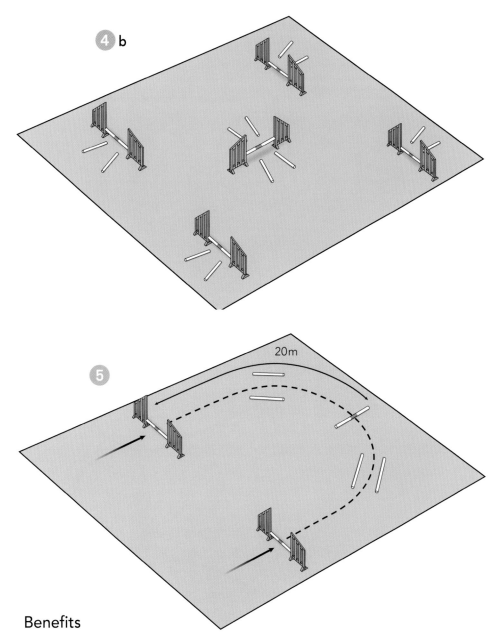

Benefits

- control of regularity
- control of direction
- patience of horse
- developing an 'eye' for canter/jump relationship.

Canter exercises with angles

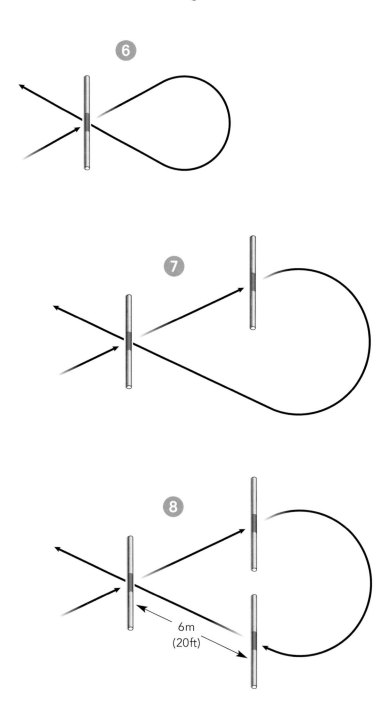

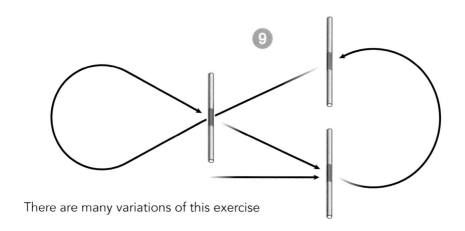

There are many variations of this exercise

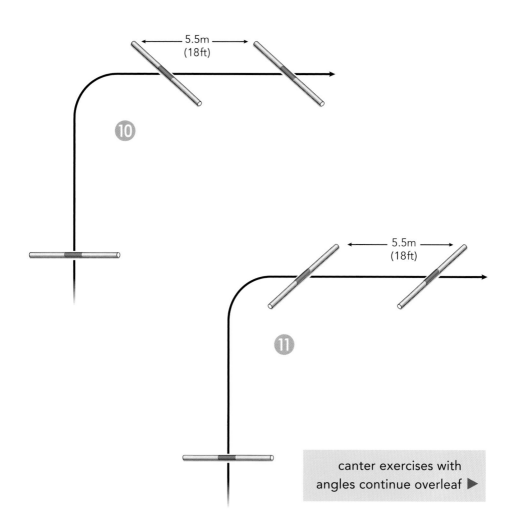

5.5m
(18ft)

5.5m
(18ft)

canter exercises with
angles continue overleaf ▶

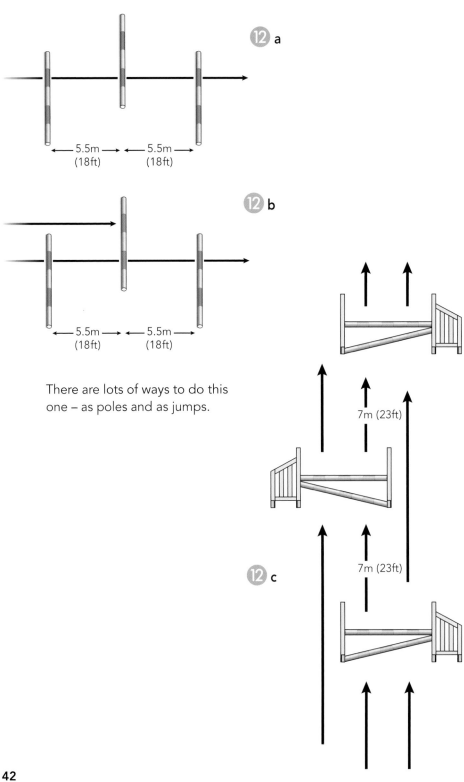

12 a

5.5m
(18ft) ← → 5.5m
(18ft)

12 b

5.5m
(18ft) ← → 5.5m
(18ft)

There are lots of ways to do this
one – as poles and as jumps.

7m (23ft)

7m (23ft)

12 c

Now challenge the partnership to ride 1, 2 or 3 strides in any distance. Many faults begin to happen.

a. Riders control from the rein, with the result the horse trots.

b. The horse loses the correctness of rhythm – loses the moment of suspension.

c. Riders lose the Balance.

There are, however, many benefits.

It's easy playing the exercise over poles on the ground. Riders develop an adjustment of canter and a feel for what they need to do to maintain the canter. They start to **take ownership** of the Pace.

Now they must become more discerning about what they feel of the Pace's quality.

Making the pole into a jump at the end of a 5/6/7/8-stride canter distance focuses the mind to ensure the canter is good enough to jump the fence. However, the good qualities of correct rhythm, regularity, straightness, balance, acceptness of the Aids and, above all, retaining forwardness must still be maintained.

It looks simple but it's not so easy. However, the rider soon develops a range of canters from small, through middle to big, each with the quality that is good enough to jump the fence and beat the course designer.

Now incorporate a curved line.

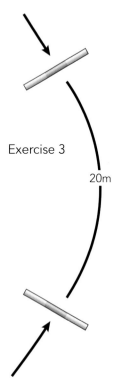

Exercise 3

20m

Exercise 3

This is the same, but now ownership with the line is being tested.

This is more challenging for the partnership. Deviation off the line changes the distances between the poles. It becomes the rider's aim to 'feel' the canter necessary to put 5, 6 or 7 strides into this distance. As they develop each canter and memorise what it feels like to produce it and hold it on the line, so another skill is learnt.

Changing Direction

Landing on the correct lead after a jump often causes concern to the rider. It need not be as troublesome as it's made out to be.

Let's take left to right.

Exercise 4

Canter left

- left leg on the girth
- right leg behind the girth
- left rein direction
- right rein controlling bend/pace.

As one approaches the jump at 90 degrees to the centre, both legs are on the girth and both reins create a neck which is in front of the rider (no bend).

Just before take off the Aids are changed for:

Canter right

- right leg on the girth
- left leg behind the girth
- right rein direction
- left rein controlling bend/pace.

On take off

- look right
- open rein right and open shoulders
- a little more weight on the right stirrup
- nudge the horse with the left leg.

Common faults to be avoided

- do *not* look down
- do *not* turn the upper body so that the weight goes to the outside.

Note the weight on the inside leg. Note the look in their eyes indicating direction. Note the inside shoulder coming back to allow the 'whole' body to 'feel' the direction of motion.

Exercise 5

There are many ways to develop this curved line now that the change of direction is mastered. Make the distances familiar to the rider. This develops a feel for the canter and a confidence in the horse. Make it clear, the number of strides being asked for. Don't leave uncertainty. The rider should be able to produce the required canter from the memory of what it feels like.

Most of the exercises can and should be done as poles on the ground or small jumps (50/60cm). They should be treated as games with a serious side to them. When teaching children or anxious adults the issues should be number of strides, holding the line, making the turn – Not the jump. Remove this as an issue and people tend to enjoy the challenges of what happens between the jumps.

Improving the **Pace** in quality, accuracy and control and then making the rider better at riding where they put the pace i.e. the **Line** has relevance in all disciplines. Relating this to dressage and show Jumping leads to less confusion between the phases.

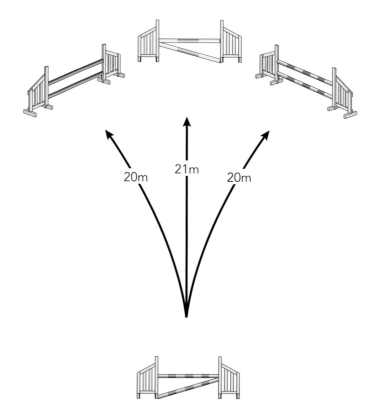

6

Handling Skills

Rein Skills

This may be a good time to introduce some simple handling skills for cross-country riding. Much time is spent in the saddle on hacks, trail riding or just being social, this time can be used to improve the handling of the reins and the use of the stick.

Knotted reins

Having one's reins knotted in the correct way can be a huge advantage for many situations. The idea is to be able to gather up the reins quickly having slipped them at a drop or a stumble, hence regaining control quickly before the next fence or to help regain balance.

Each rider will tend to have their preferred type of cross-country reins. Some are easier to knot than others. *See* the examples on page 50.

Many riders will say, 'I can't ride with my reins so short'. My answer is, 'learn'. The benefits are huge and it's just practice and getting used to it. One needs to practise the method of gathering them up in the space of one stride, so that this becomes second nature – no thought, as shown in the two pictures on page 51.

The Stick/Whip

We are all one-sided as riders. We get used to carrying a stick or whip in the same hand, however, it is important to be ambidextrous. The stick or whip can be of huge value as an extra Aid to help the control of Line.

A tap on the outside shoulder can close an escape route, encourage the horse to follow the inside rein as well as sharpen his reaction if need be.

We need to practise changing it from one hand to the other when we are cantering and galloping. Jockeys are expert at it, because it's in their interest. It is also in our interest, so it's a skill worth spending some time on.

right and *below* Examples of knotted reins

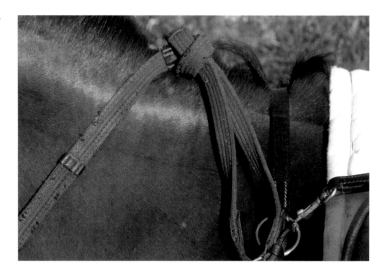

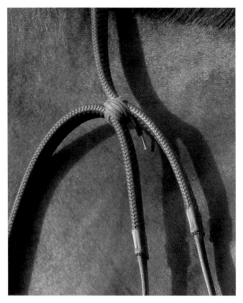

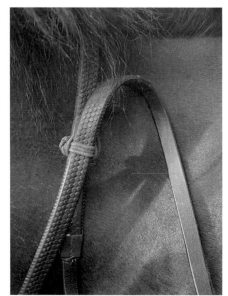

Good balance

One stride later … ready
for the next jump

7

Ownership Responsibilities

I have already used the expression 'the rider *own*s the canter'. Let's explore this statement a little more. In many ways this focuses on the most important part of cross-country riding – who does what.

The rider's job is to look after the **Pace** and **Line**. It's the horse's job to look after the **Jump**.

Read the above sentence ten times!

Up to now we have taught exercises for the riders and horses to improve the canter and where they are going. Direction should be the responsibility of the rider; after all they are the only member of the partnership who knows where they are going. The rider knows what is ahead and what questions are there to be answered. This should allow them to prepare the pace and line necessary to solve the problem the course designer has set – whether it be dressage, show jumping or cross-country.

The horse's job is to listen to the rider and respond accordingly. However, when a jump appears the responsibilities should change, as the horse now becomes responsible and the rider supportive. If we have trained the horse to understand that at some stage before a jump the rider will begin passing responsibility to it, then it will begin to take more interest in what the jump is and how they negotiate it.

Whilst jumping combinations, related distances or directional lines it is still the rider's job to determine line and pace, the horse will continue jumping whatever is on the line in front of him.

When the jump is over, the horse relinquishes the responsible role and is again guided by the rider as far as pace and line are concerned.

When jumping, the rider is hugely supportive of the horse's efforts but the horse must initiate the jumping process. This allows the horse to jump with understanding and responsibility for getting safely to the other side.

So how do we teach this process?

Look ... Jump

To teach and encourage the correct response to happen at a jump it is important to understand the aim. A horse must assess what they have to do to negotiate the obstacle; it is, after all, their responsibility. This assessment takes time. How much time is different for experienced and inexperienced, for young and old.

It is, however, important to encourage horses to become familiar with this process of Look ... Jump.

The horse that look-jumps with no pause is too hurried and cannot assess. The horse that dwells too much on the pause will lose momentum, impulsion and sometimes the desire to jump at all. So the timing of the pause is critical. It must be a fluid movement of look ... pause ... jump.

The horse that jumps without looking is not safe and should not be ridden further.

Having developed a balanced canter and the idea of maintaining regularity, now canter to a small jump (50cm approx.). Don't look for a 'spot', a stride, a take off, 3.2.1 etc. just keep your canter.

This is harder to do than one thinks. It is human nature to 'want to do something'. Don't. Most horses will expect help and guidance – give them none other than staying on line.

The horse's options:

a. Meet the jump at a nice spot to take off.

b. Get too close.

c. Be too far away.

d. Stop.

If **a.** happens, good, reward and repeat the process because it may have been lucky!

If **b.** happens and the horse makes a good decision, by being quick to balance and push off the front legs to avoid hitting the jump, good. Reward and repeat the process. If not, and he knocks the jump, repeat the process but still don't help him.

If **c.** happens and the horse takes off, they have made a decision, reward him and go again.

If **d.** happens, go again from a good canter, most likely the horse was waiting to be told to jump and failed to make a decision himself.

As we canter over this jump anything up to six or seven times, without telling the horse when to jump, you will find the horse beginning to take responsibility (ownership) of what to do. He will begin to 'measure' his approach to put himself on a spot from which a jump is safe and economical. The rider must continue to support the horse whilst this process is taking place. The canter must remain consistent in quality and line.

Before long the jump will become rounder and the horse will be more confident.

The trainer must allow this process to happen without commenting on right or wrong take-offs, strides or spots. This only makes the rider more anxious. Keep the focus on balance, canter, line and any other subject but the jump. Over a period of time you will find that the rider will adopt the quality of the canter and line as the main priority and the horse will adopt the jump as his main priority.

During the recognised five phases of a jump the responsibilities go something like this:

Approach: Rider beginning to hand over to the horse/pony some 20m away from jump.

Take off: Rider ensuring the horse/pony is making a decision and being supportive of it.

In the air: Rider in balance supporting the horse's/pony's efforts.

Landing: As above.

Get away: Rider regaining the role of directing proceedings, of line and pace.

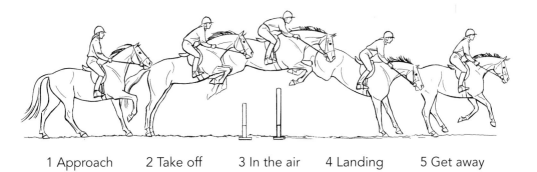

1 Approach   2 Take off   3 In the air   4 Landing   5 Get away

Some horses like to be close to a jump, others a little off the jump. The horse must be allowed to make that decision. For the horse that *doesn't* make a decision, the rider must reprimand and then repeat the process, being careful not to make the decision for the horse. Remember we are trying to encourage the horse to take that responsibility.

> For me, this is one of the most important parts of risk management and safer cross-country riding. For riders that have difficulty in seeing where they are in front of a fence it allows them to go with confidence, that the horse is helping them and not waiting to be told.

This process begins in the school where the jumps knock down and the concept can be taught without any risk to horse or rider. Bring the process outside with you.

8

Outside Jumping

Confirm the ability to ride a balanced and controlled canter in the open space. Open spaces tend to encourage horses to be more unruly and riders more carefree. Begin in a small field or the corner of a field before venturing into the big open space.

Practise turns and transitions to ensure control. Once this is done and the partnership is reminded of their responsibilities jumping can commence.

The first log or small vertical reminds the horse, and rider of what is expected. This can be done from trot or canter. Everything done in the school applies in the country.

As a coach/trainer focus on the Pace and Line not the jump at this stage. The jump will happen because the Pace and Line are good. The rider then becomes less preoccupied with the jump.

There are many exercises that can be used for ponies and horses at the lower level which can be adapted for the more advanced partnership.

Exercise 1

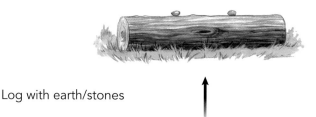

Log with earth/stones

Each turn into the jump has its issues.

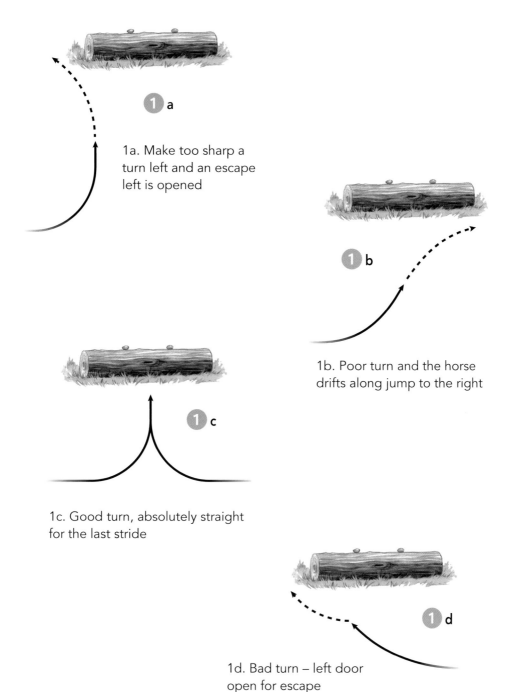

1a. Make too sharp a turn left and an escape left is opened

1b. Poor turn and the horse drifts along jump to the right

1c. Good turn, absolutely straight for the last stride

1d. Bad turn – left door open for escape

These targets on a log can be continually changed to keep the focus on Line and Pace and not the jump.

Honesty to a Line

In dressage we are asked to ride shapes and lines testing our ability to communicate with a horse. When the horse can stay between the left and right aids we can confidently ride centre lines and circles. It's the same cross-country schooling. This develops a quality of honesty to a line where the horse stays on the line until given the signal to change lines. This is good to teach now as it becomes more important later on in their education.

Confirm the honesty

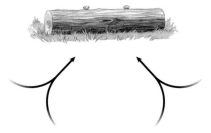

Each of these approaches tests the rider and horse's ability to hold a line. Some riders and horses are better one side than the other. Both must be practised until the skills are equal on both reins.

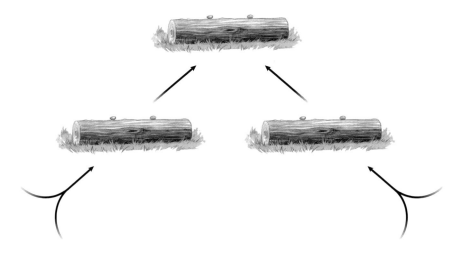

When this exercise is mastered the landing and getaway are now challenged.

To drift off the line between the logs:

a. Changes the distance.

b. Opens escape routes.

It's important to remember that up to now we have done lots of jumping, which most pupils want, but nothing is challenging or focusing specifically on the jump. It is purely Pace and Line, allowing this concept to become ingrained in the subconscious.

Escape Routes

To talk about escape routes is not being negative, it's being realistic, as they exist. All cross-country riders walk courses looking for them to enable their lines and approaches to give the horse the best opportunity of jumping the jump and avoiding the escape routes. Most horses have a preferred way of drifting, often opening up an escape route. This can be identified when trotting or cantering over a pole on the ground. As trainers and riders we should be aware of the horse's favoured side, or drift, to enable us to school it out and make both sides even. (Beware, in a moment of crisis it may appear.)

Undulating Ground and Gradients

Undulating ground provides many challenges for both horse and rider. Much can be done to improve the balance and control of the partnership whilst also incorporating jumps.

Always 'go with' not 'against' the ground.

Galloping over the ground, the horse is the expert. That's what they do naturally. They will choose the best speed and often line to negotiate a piece of ground. As riders, we need to go with the horse by remaining in balance and support their efforts by leg and rein contact.

Riders often feel that horses go too fast downhill. Remember they have four legs to provide their balance, we have only two. Going uphill we need to stay as near their centre of gravity as possible in order to make it easier for them to push. *See* the illustrations below.

Now incorporate the same exercises as before, (1a to 1d on page 57) with the ups and downs as approaches and getaways. This imposes new challenges to the control of pace and line.

Uphill and downhill, horse and rider

Continue to teach, ride and learn that a good line and balance will create the situation that the horse can jump from. Out of balance or off line and the jump becomes unpredictable.

Gallop to Canter

Cross-country is based on crossing the country at the most economical speed but trying to be under the optimum time if possible. Every second counts.

Stop, start cross-country is exhausting for the horse and produces the picture of show jumping in the country. To go from a gallop to a canter with ease and no apparent change to the balance or regularity of pace, has to be the aim. This requires practise and should be incorporated at this stage into the jump games.

Horses in gallop should accept and understand the Aids just as much as when they are in canter or jump mode. We need to teach gallop just as much as any other gait. Horses are not natural gallopers, they are born sprinters. A quick burst is used to get away from danger (fright and flight).

The same qualities apply as in dressage or jumping:

- forward not speed
- regularity
- acceptance and understanding of the Aids
- contact not too strong
- self carriage
- balance.

The transition from gallop to jumping canter requires the rider to subtly change his position. The upper body is raised, simultaneously the lower leg closes and the reins restrain, i.e. the half halt, or rebalance within the pace. Having made the transition it is important to continue taking the canter forward to the jump, as to dwell on the transition wastes precious time and the canter quickly loses momentum. *See* the photo overleaf.

The rebalance

Judgement of Speed

How often is it said that the good riders have a 'built in clock'. Whilst inside the time they never seem to be hurrying. This is a practised skill, not luck. Begin the process with the young horse and rider – both need to understand the process.

The horse

Canter in balance accepting and understanding the aids at 400 metres per minute over a measured distance, say 1200 metres (i.e. 3 minutes). When this becomes easy, up the speed to 450 metres per minute and the time becomes 2 minutes 40 seconds. This too must become easy, i.e. not hurried.

Go again at 475 metres per minute, therefore 2 minutes 31 seconds, then 500 metres per minute therefore 2 minutes 24 seconds.

It may take some time to develop a quiet easy gallop with the horse going within himself.

The rider

Begin with a horse that knows its job and will maintain its regularity. Again, start at 400 metres per minute for 1200 metres, the rider must be within one or two seconds plus or minus of the 3 minutes. This must not be achieved by speeding up or slowing down towards the end. The coach can monitor this with measured markers, giving help on where time was lost or gained.

Same again with 450, 475 and then 500 metres per minute with appropriate times of 2 minutes 40 seconds, 2 minutes 31 seconds and 2 minutes 24 seconds. With repetition the mind begins to 'feel' the speed and relate it to metres per minute.

Now we link the gallop to jump transition, and the above exercise of judgement of speeds.

In the same 1200 metre distance put three simple jumps and repeat the exercise for horse and rider. What will happen the first few times, is that the rider will go too slowly for the jump and too quickly between the jumps. The coach must try to encourage a smooth transition from gallop to canter, as early as possible, to allow the horse time to take ownership of the jump and as late as possible to save time with a smooth return to gallop after the jump.

Use the same speed variables and allow plenty of practice time to ensure this skill becomes a habit. More jumps can be used as the competence improves but up to six is plenty.

Remember to practise both reins!

Uphill and Downhill

Balance is always easier uphill than downhill. However, there are other important considerations. Course designers will site jumps on hills to test a number of important qualities:

- balance

- control

- impulsion

- confidence.

When jumping uphill, horses tend to balance themselves, especially if the rider supports their efforts. To do this the rider moves their centre of gravity forward, freeing up the horse's hindquarters and back, to allow them to push. Encouragement from the rider's leg aids and support through contact with the reins will put the horse into the best possible frame for jumping uphill.

The horse will naturally shorten its stride and measure the fence, as it decides where to take off. The further away from the jump the higher it becomes. They will tend to go close.

Impulsion is vital. The creation and control of this energy is important. Too little, and the jump becomes imposing. Speed, and the jump

Uphill

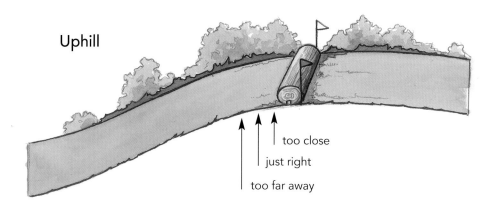

too close

just right

too far away

Downhill

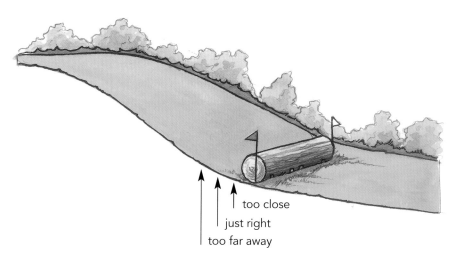

too close

just right

too far away

becomes flat. A flat jump creates difficulty in gaining height and hence insufficient time for the front legs to unfold and prepare for landing.

To practise this, having already ridden undulations, is fairly straight-forward. Small logs or tree trunks on a mound are a good start. Encourage the 'feel' of an engaged, slightly shorter but positively forward canter. Initially riders will either be too far forward or behind the movement. The former could lead to a stop. The latter, to the rider being pushed forward over the jump which often leads to an uncomfortable two or three strides after the jump. Some fresh horses take advantage of this imbalance to buck … so beware.

Downhill too has its issues. With four legs doing what nature intended they normally cope very well, however, we must assist them with a secure lower leg, encouraging engagement *not* chasing speed, a supportive contact, *not* allowing speed but *not* fighting.

Left alone, the stride tends to become bigger downhill. To jump successfully we must ensure that it stays balanced and of normal length.

The take-off in relation to the fence will be better if it is a little off rather than too deep. Downhill will tend to draw the horse into the base of the jump which often creates a challenge for the front leg technique.

Hold, support and encourage the horse to make a quick decision.

Again a log or tree trunk are good training jumps. They tend to be forgiving of mistakes by horse or rider, so facilitate learning.

9

How to Teach

Steps

Steps both up and down are a good test of the balance and gymnastic ability of the partnership. The choice of canter and position of the rider is crucial.

The up step

Chosen first as it tends to be easier to teach, the up step should be small. This allows the horse to understand what it must do to negotiate the test. Knowing how to coordinate their movement will be vital later on, so a good start is important. Gymnastic exercises, in the school, such as bounce exercises are helpful to both horse and rider.

The canter must be engaged, not long and flat. Too short often leads to a lack of momentum which makes it difficult for the horse.

The rider must:

- **sit up** … stay light in the seat

- **look up** … where they want to go

- **get up** … be positive to maintain momentum.

Remember: it is physically quite hard for horses to jump up and take you with them.

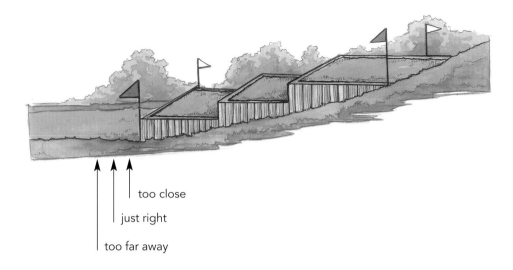

too close

just right

too far away

Too close – challenging to technique and loss of momentum.

Too far – a flat jump with many difficulties?

a. Hind legs often don't make the step.

b. The second step is hard for the horse to get height.

c. The third step loses momentum.

The down step

Managing gravity: when horses are in balance and between the aids, they manage gravity very well. So the key is again to choose a canter or trot that is in control and looking. Start on small steps to allow the horse to understand how to coordinate their legs and balance. The rider supports with secure leg aids and a good contact. Control of speed is vital – too fast and gravity takes over, making it difficult for the horse to co-ordinate leg movement.

The rider must sit in the *middle* of the horse. Too far forward places weight on the forehand, again making it difficult for the horse. Too far back and the momentum is often lost, which can create control issues in the first few strides after the steps.

High jump ... vs ... long jump

For the most part eventers are high jumpers. Most of their jumping efforts require a bascule (i.e. where the horse rounds its top line as in the top picture). There are very few jumps where long and flat is acceptable.

Develop the ability to produce a canter or gallop that allows the horse to jump up and round, *not* long and flat. Most horses will choose to do this given the correct approach.

A round cross-country jump

A flat steeplechaser jump

Banks

These can be quite disruptive to the flow of a course. They take time and therefore increase the need to up the speed between fences. The quicker we can negotiate them the better. In order to do this safely and economically we must practise the skill.

A strong, uphill canter is required for a horse to jump up. Carrying the rider is an effort and there may be other jumping efforts linked to the bank so it can become quite physically demanding.

Practise the skill of jumping up and remaining in balance before linking it to the approach or getaway.

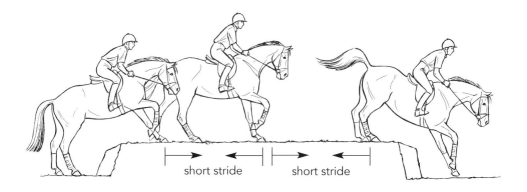

short stride   short stride

Note the rider position on approach and landing

Pace – strong, uphill, canter. Not a flat gallop!

The rider should be quick to go from slightly behind, to up and with the horse, in order that balance and momentum are maintained. Once the partnership grasps the skills then the approach and getaway must be thought about.

To go from a gallop to a canter or a jumping gallop is a very important skill to learn for the rider and also to teach every horse. The rebalance from one pace to another must be clear and understood.

- Close legs… beside the girth indicates to the horse/pony to engage his hind legs under his body.

- Hold both reins… means 'steady' not so fast as I'm trying to change your balance onto your hind legs.

- Sit up ... bringing the head up, shoulders back and seat closer to the saddle brings the weight back.

All this happens at once and must produce a response from the horse.

The horse must learn this rebalance just as much as the rider. The later it can happen on the approach the more the galloping speed can be maintained. Therefore, the more time-efficient one becomes. However, leave it too late and the preparation for the jump may be hindered.

The landing or getaway from a fence or bank is also key to getting back into galloping mode and hence saving time. Jumping up a bank will shorten the first stride of the bank and having jumped off the first two strides will also be short. Encourage the horse to 'jump off' rather than 'drop off'.

Don't dwell on the first three strides after the bank or jump, inwardly congratulating oneself on a job well done, that's two seconds wasted. Don't land and chase the horse as this will be interpreted by the horse as 'what's wrong?' Land ... and ... reward ... and ... gallop ... back into the speed you were in before the bank or jump.

Drops

When does a drop become a drop? For me, when it requires slipping the reins. *See* the photo opposite.

Going from one level to another does not always require the skills or adjustment of balance that a drop does. It is not possible to put a measurement on this, as the size of the horse has a part to play.

The skill of slipping reins can and should be practised when out for a hack, when there is plenty of time to become adept in what to do. Make it such a habit that no thought is required on its execution. (*See* paragraph on page 49 on rein skills.)

Again, speed must be controlled. Sufficient forward momentum must be maintained to allow the horse to look – jump – seeing clearly where he is to land. Often too much time to look will result in a step back or stop.

Never practise large drops; it is unnecessary. The adrenalin of competition will make it happen. Too much practice can be jarring on the front legs and shoulders, which will ultimately discourage horses from jumping drops.

Ready for the next jump...two strides later

Bullfinches

Horses do need to believe that it is safe for them to take off and that the landing is also safe to receive them. A bullfinch challenges this belief hence testing the courage and confidence of the horse and its training.

Begin with a small brush and only a few wisps of tall brush. Here the horse can see clearly that it is ok. Do not overdo the density of the wisps as it then encourages horses to jump over the whole thing. Quite thrilling at times but it can easily frighten a horse with the result that it may be reluctant to 'have a go' next time.

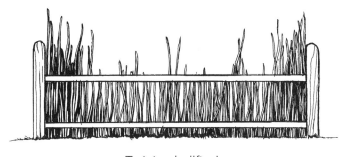

Training bullfinch

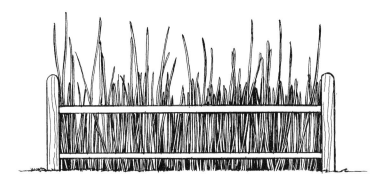

Competition bullfinch

In competition, riders should beware of the next jump after a bull-finch. Horses often become wary of the question and produce a less than confident jump. The result can be a gradual erosion of the horse's confidence. Feel it happening and be quick to repair the uncertainty by taking an alternative which may be an easier option. Don't be too proud to do this!

The 'feel good factor' in practise

Water Jumps

One of the most important jumps for which to be thorough in your training. A good grounding, building lots of confidence, will last a life-time. Do it wrong and it will come back to haunt you.

Instinctively horses drink water but they tend not to be 'water babies'. Introduced to water correctly they can come to love it as can be seen by the pictures of horses swimming and sporting in the sea and rivers. The natural caution is two fold: fear of predators and uncertain footing.

When planning a training session do your homework. A first-timer will need a good water facility and preferably a schoolmaster friend who 'does' water well. A rehab situation will need the same and may also need the help of a lunge line and perhaps more than one schoolmaster. The experienced ones will just enjoy themselves.

The principle is:

walk in, walk out

walk in, trot out

trot in, trot out

trot in, canter out etc.

Now the two natural fears have been dispelled.

(The beach, if available is great for giving horses confidence in water. Becoming used to cantering in shallow water with the resultant splashing removes another concern. Be careful though as some beaches have uncertain footing; therefore know your beach and don't go fast. Normally the water in the first 8 to 10 feet (3 metres) of the sea will produce good footing in the sand.)

Trot and jump out over a log or up a small bank/step first before attempting to jump into water. Make sure the trot has impulsion and that the horse jumps up and out. (*See* Steps and Banks.)

Then canter in water and introduce a small jump out. Make sure the rider leaves the horse to make its own decision when to jump. Often they will make a mistake when learning, either stumbling up without jumping or, launching themselves from far away and not making a comfortable jump. Either way, repeat the same exercise, supporting their efforts and you will be surprised how quickly they learn where to put their own feet.

Jumping in always causes more concern. Here the rider has to be more awake and ready to assist as the timing of that assistance is critical. Choose a small step in, one that could be walked. Following the schoolmaster at a good positive trot support the horse as it looks … jump.

The 'look' part must not become prolonged. The rider must be quick to encourage with leg and voice and maybe a slap behind the girth with the stick. (Not a punishment but a slap.) The timing of this is important as all too often when the look is prolonged the horse then decides not to go. The horse's eyes and ears and body language will help the rider to support and encourage at the right time.

Don't overdo the height or complexity of this first session of jumping

The positive look!

in. Leave the horse with a positive and confident attitude because of a good experience. Then the next time will be easier. We must be prepared to do this training often at the early stages, as **total** confidence must be established, if we don't want a ghost to appear later on.

More complex water jumping can then be developed. Don't challenge with height until the mind can work through the questions. Keep the jumps trotable and far enough apart until the mind copes. *See* the diagrams on the following page.

As the horse grows in confidence it will solve problems better. It will then become better at co-ordination:

- mental, i.e solving the problem

- physical, i.e. using its jumping technique.

When both work together well you have a good water jumper.

The same can be said of the rider. The rider has to learn where and how to stay in balance as well as the timing of support. Anticipation of what the horse is likely to do is a great help to the rider being in the

Out of water

3 strides

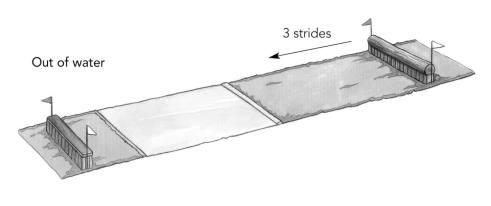

Edge of water

2 strides

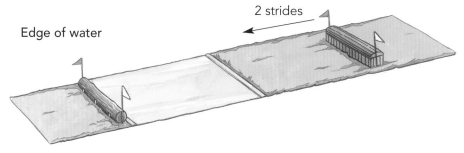

Examples of more complex
water jumps

Into the water

1 stride

2 strides

1 stride

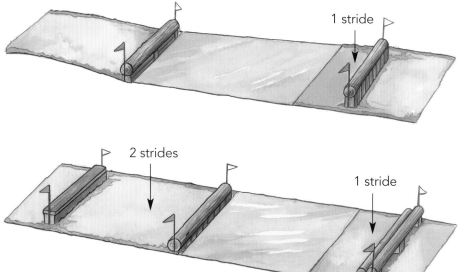

right place:

- in front of the movement can produce a stop

- behind the movement tends to produce an awkward jump with the resultant bad 'feel'/'experience' for the horse.

Water tends to slow a horse down, therefore the rider should be aware of this and avoid being in front of the movement.

Practising the skills of being light, and quick to slip and then shorten the reins will help balance, and the confidence of the partnership.

Ditches

A very important subject to teach well. All too often we hear parents and pupils say how good their horse or pony is across the country but that it has a 'thing' about ditches. Taught well they need never have a 'thing' about ditches, but often we, as instructors, are left to rehabilitate the 'dodgy ditch jumper'.

Let's start from a clean sheet. The horse who has never seen a ditch before, *never* give them *any* doubt. The seed of doubt will grow to haunt you in years to come, so don't sow it. Begin with undulating ground and places where the horses are encouraged to look down at their footing. This will start the process of having confidence in where they are putting their feet. Find a *really* small ditch, almost a dry gully like the one in the pictured overleaf. Help from a horse that 'goes' is useful. Walk or trot over this, being aware that the first time of asking is crucial. To over ride (not speed) is almost better than under ride. You can apologise when you are on the other side.

Take your time in making this experience so secure and comfortable in the horse's mind that it is the foundation for the future. Never be tempted to do something too big for the stage of training.

It is important that they look…jump, because to understand what is being asked of them is vital. This eliminates any fear of the unknown.

Trainers should note the way their pupils' horses jump ditches as it gives them a clue as to what is to come in the future. The horse that jumps 'flat' and is keen to 'get to the other side' may lack scope and confidence. This 'flying low' may prove to be a limiting factor later on with trakheners and wide ditches as the horse's personal limits are found. The horse that jumps up and round in a good bascule will be good over ditches and trakheners and will tend to have more scope in the future.

As confidence grows the horse *must* be allowed to find its own 'confident spot' to take off from.

Prepared ditch

Unprepared ditch

The Trakhener

This obstacle seldom causes a problem if we've done our homework over a ditch. Again, the building of total confidence at the early stages is vital, we want *no* seeds of doubt. Plan these early stages for horse and rider well. Go to places that do have small and inviting jumps. Don't get tempted once you arrive to do something too big or without proper preparation. *You will regret it!*

If possible in the early stages the front of the ditch should be covered.

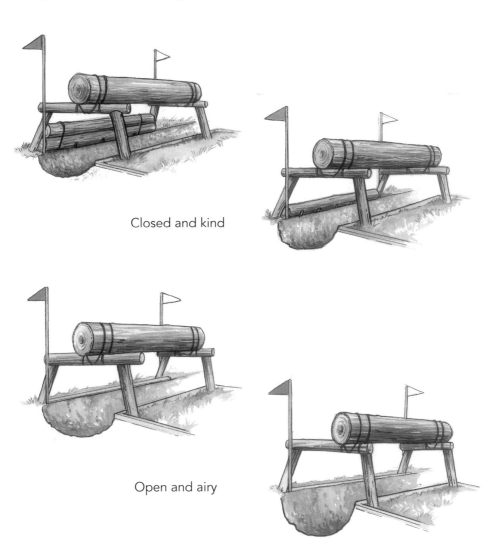

Closed and kind

Open and airy

Canters should be strong but not fast. Don't look too much for where you are in front of the jump. The face of the ditch is a natural ground line and gives the horse all the information it needs to take off. The rider retains the contact through the rein, supports with the leg aids and looks well beyond the landing. Job done.

Never worry if the horse 'stutters' a short stride in on take-off. If the pace is right, this is often better for the jump as it gives the horse the opportunity to look...jump and see where it's landing.

Combinations

These can take on many different styles and degrees of difficulty. It is where the cross-country course designer can test the rider's control and the horse's physical and mental gymnastic ability.

When teaching both horse and rider it is important to remember, never over-face either, but always retain the willingness to 'have a go' and 'solve the problem'. With this in mind, as always keep the jumps low and the questions simple to start with. When horses get accustomed to problem-solving and their success rate grows, so the training can challenge more.

The skill of holding a line and pace over a series of poles and small jumps has already been practised. Begin making these more challenging. *See* the two examples opposite.

Centre line is one stride between each element. This becomes very challenging to control line and pace.

The use of terrain changes the difficulty of jumps, so too in combinations. A simple layout can become quite difficult when ups and downs are introduced. Camber (across a slope) is even more challenging to holding a chosen route.

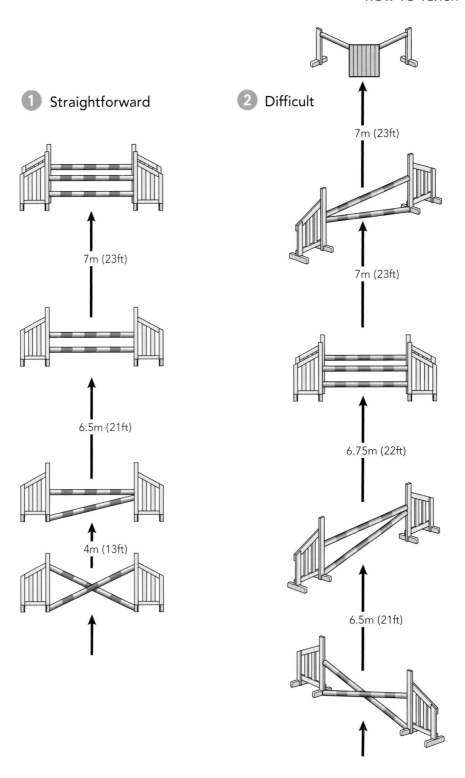

① Straightforward

7m (23ft)

6.5m (21ft)

4m (13ft)

② Difficult

7m (23ft)

7m (23ft)

6.75m (22ft)

6.5m (21ft)

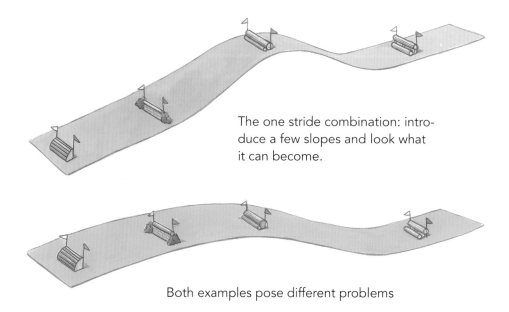

The one stride combination: introduce a few slopes and look what it can become.

Both examples pose different problems

Remember

- keep the jumps low

- piece the problems together bit by bit

- skill development takes time

- confidence must be retained

- the horse *must* learn to solve the problem.

As the course designer increases the degree of difficulty the rider must be taught how to 'think through' a combination. If the rider cannot see his way through you can be sure the horse won't either.

Once horses grow in confidence and begin to look down the line the rider is steering them, they start to 'lock on' to the jumps to be negotiated. The partnership will tend to be more in control at element **A** than the last element. This will mean a greater risk can be taken at the first element in order to make the last one easier.

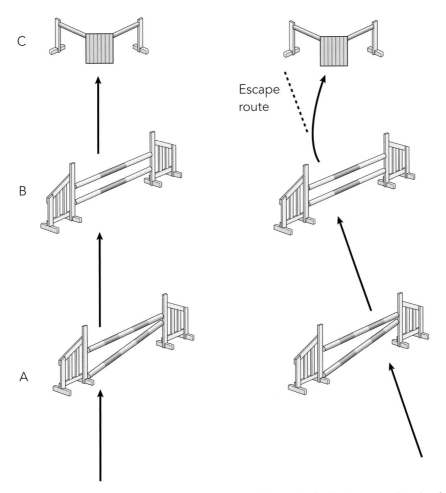

Example 1. Harder start, easier finish

Example 2. Easier start, harder finish

Corners, Arrowheads and Skinnies

The initial homework for these is best done in the arena.

The very first time we take our horse over a pole on the ground most horses will display a tendency to drift right or left. **Take note**. This will be their favoured way of drifting and tends to remain with them throughout their life. We may 'school' this out of them, to some extent, but when the pressure is on and instinct takes over, it will reappear.

Having schooled the concept of 'line' over a single pole and then a small vertical, it is time to introduce a corner.

83

Corners

The theory ...

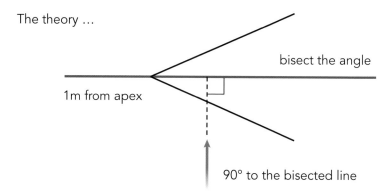

When training, make it so simple that the thought of deviation off the line is just unthinkable. Create boundaries to guide and direct the line. Remember, the habit of jumping straight doesn't happen with just one or two correct jumps.

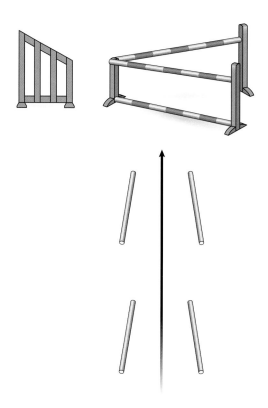

Practise right- and left-handed corners. Practise right- and left-handed corners off the right and left reins. Practise right- and left-handed corners off the right and left canter lead. Each way will pose new and different issues for your horse and possibly your riding. Most riders are one sided and favour right or left. Practise correcting your weakness.

The end result: straight and honest

Arrowheads

As we continue to *develop honesty to the line*, arrowheads and other skinny fences must be practised. The classic arrowhead is:

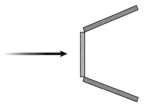

It has degrees of angle and difficulty of profile.

In schooling, it is important to build and develop the honesty. Making the angle very small is the start.

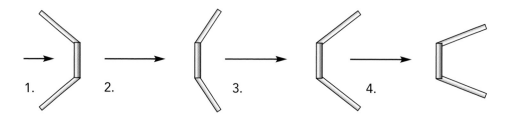

Again, boundaries on the approach and getaway are helpful to the development of staying on line.

When horses begin to feel that the exercises are too challenging, tension will show itself in many forms: through the rein, drift, poor technique, running out etc. If you have hurried the process be quick to retrace your steps and rebuild the confidence.

Skinnies

A similar technique is adopted when teaching 'skinnies' (single narrow fences). Focus on line and close escape routes. *See* diagram opposite.

The horse should *want to take you to the fence*, rather than look for the an escape route. When they do you know it is time to ask a little more.

Practise off the right and left rein. Practise off a turn, right and left.

The canter adopted should be a slightly shorter and more engaged one, as this puts the take-off closer to the jump thus eliminating the escape routes.

Give yourself a target 'spot' one stride away from the jump, as you need to be at 90 degrees to the centre of the jump. This will tighten up your riding, speed up the horse's reaction time, improve honesty and save some vital seconds on the course. *See* diagram opposite.

Feel for any drift right or left as you are now exposing the horse's weakness. School to make it better by reducing the difficulty of the exercise therefore only challenging the line, not making the jump the challenge.

Now take some poles and uprights outside and school in the natural terrain. Undulating ground changes the difficulty and challenges the horse and rider more. **Keep the challenge being the line and pace not**

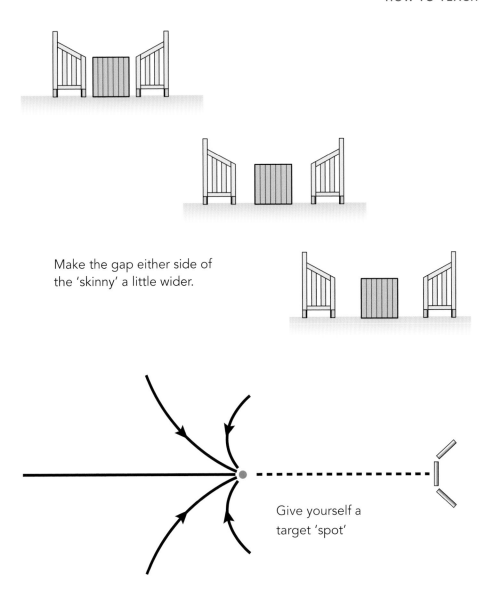

Make the gap either side of
the 'skinny' a little wider.

Give yourself a
target 'spot'

the height of the fence. We continue to want the horse to look for and
want to jump between the flags.

The course designer will set tests of control and balance, uphill and
downhill, off turns and straight lines, in combinations and single
fences, off banks and before banks. We must recreate as many of these
as possible.

We are asking horses to problem-solve. Therefore, don't over-face
the mind. Make the fence simple and low as it then keeps the horse

87

confident in its ability to solve the problem. It makes the instinctive process clear and so improves co-ordination and hence performance.

When using related distances, i.e. off a bank to a skinny, initially make the distance generous. By using a 3- or 4-stride distance the horse and rider have time to regroup between elements. This allows them to piece the combination together, element by element, and so improve their problem-solving.

Bounces

These are often used in a schooling situation or as part of a grid (gymnastic jumping). It is a valid cross-country question in the correct situation and therefore needs to be practised.

Gymnastically it is quite difficult for a horse to jump in over the first element and take off again before the back feet have even touched the ground. This is called a bounce. In order for a horse to negotiate this type of jump successfully it needs to have practice in learning how to co-ordinate its jumping action.

The coach needs to help the rider find a suitable canter so that the horse has time and is in balance to make the bounce possible.

Trotting to a small double of cross-poles is a good start. They should be 10–11 feet (3m approx) apart. When the horse negotiates this with ease, then make them two small verticals, 2 feet (60cm) in height and 10–11 feet (3m) apart. The canter required is a short 'punchy' canter with lots of impulsion. The rider must not get in front of the movement on the approach, the upper body is quite upright. On take-off the rider must support the horse's efforts by retaining a contact and being positive with the leg contact. The rider's position through the exercises must remain in balance and flexible at the ankle and knee, whilst being light of the seat and retaining the contact through the rein.

The next process that requires attention is the transition from a bold or faster canter to a shorter more punchy canter. *See* the diagram on page opposite .

This practice can now be taken into the cross-country field. Remember to keep the jumps small and ensure the transition to a shorter more controlled canter happens. This will allow the horse time to look... jump and the speed has been reduced to balance the take-off.

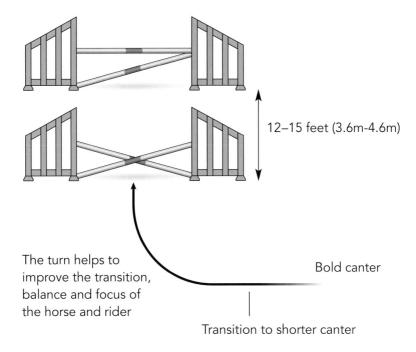

12–15 feet (3.6m-4.6m)

The turn helps to improve the transition, balance and focus of the horse and rider

Bold canter

Transition to shorter canter

Verticals

The ability to jump a vertical, like a gate, at cross-country speed is a skill that needs to be practised. Ground lines and dressing have softened the profile of the vertical so that in recent times it has ceased to be a vertical! The type and quality of canter is critical to negotiating a true vertical.

Seldom will this fence be found at the end of a straight or after a long gallop. It is more likely to be off a turn or in a controlled part of the course.

In a similar way to the preparation for a bounce, the transition from gallop to canter is important. A shorter more engaged pace is required. In riding the turn, the horse must develop an improved balance. The rider will close the seat to the saddle and sit a little more upright (I do not mean a deep seat or sit back).

To help train the horse to jump verticals, place a pole out from the base of the jump about 60cm. This will develop his eye and where he should take off.

To help train the rider the canter exercise 5 on page 39 is very useful.

Hidden Landings

Any jump with a hidden landing requires thought and an understanding of what the issues are and how they are to be resolved. When horses cannot see where they are landing there is an understandable concern. Often they only see this landing during or after they have taken off. To teach both the horse and rider, it is important the trainer is aware of this and understands how to deal with the resulting issues.

- **The horse**...the canter needs to be energetic, punchy and short. Being shorter allows for a take-off area closer to the fence, being punchy and energetic will encourage a quicker 'ground tapping' take-off. This is important as the horse's front legs and shoulder action need to be good, as often on take-off the horse is distracted by the uncertainty of landing and hence becomes lazy in this action. It is vital for a safe landing that the front legs are 'clear' over the obstacle; back legs may and often do drag a little. This dragging can be of help as it can slow down this follow-through, easing the landing.

  The horse at all times needs the rider's *committed support* through leg and rein. The horse must never feel abandoned.

- **The rider**...must plan the transition from gallop to canter giving enough time for the horse to assess the question and prepare the answer.

The often named 'coffin canter' is chosen. This is an energetic and punchy canter with the horse off his forehand. The rider's position must be encouraged to be a light seat, but the upper body quite upright, the leg should be secure and a little forward.

Commitment and support are part of the rider's role in encouraging the horse to jump whilst not altogether knowing where the landing is. Getting the front end to work is vital. Gymnastic exercises in the school will help. Confidence-building cross-country schooling will continue to build the horse's trust in the rider's request and also develop the correct response reflex.

Common faults

Fault	Result
• not enough impulsion	– horse/pony stops
• too fast	– challenging to front leg technique – lands too far down – loss of balance and control on take-off and landing
• canter too big	– take off too close, challenging the technique again – take-off too far away resulting in a flattening of the jump just at the moment the horse is distracted looking for its landing.

All of these results are classic fall scenarios.

Riding Turns

Often this skill is left unpractised. It is vital to give your horse the best approach possible to the jump.

The Aids have been explained on earlier pages. Now refine their meaning. The inside leg *does not* need to push the horse out … unless it has fallen in. It is there to guide the horse on to the chosen line.

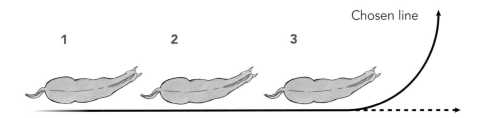

1. Inside rein asks for bend.
Inside leg stops the fall left and pushes the horse along the line.
Outside rein allows for bend but also says 'don't go there yet'.
Outside leg guides and looks after the outside of the horse.

2. As above but the horse and rider have had the opportunity to prepare themselves for the turn because they know its going to happen, they are also looking towards the new line and possible jump.

3. On reaching the turn the outside rein allows the horse to go in the direction it is looking, and is encouraged to do so by the outside leg actively saying 'go to where the inside rein is guiding'.

Outside leg to inside rein

The more horses get used to being 'positioned' before the turn the easier they find the turn, when they are actually asked for it. This forewarning assists the horse's own preparation.

More educated partnerships can make the turns more challenging. For example.

90–180 degree turns can be 'towards' a canter pirouette

The outside rein becomes more assertive in saying *wait*.

The inside leg engages the horse's inside hind leg, creating more balance.

The outside leg just behind the girth asks the forehand to move over, to follow the directional inside rein.

Practise this at walk, trot and canter in the school, around and between jumps and also when jumping. It will allow the partnership to develop a keener eye for the quickest and most economical route to the jump.

Riding turns in this way is a positive way of going cross country and should be encouraged by the instructor. It can save time and allows for prepared and smooth riding. The expression to learn is: **Follow the Lead Rein.**

Bending Lines

Teaching bending lines can be fun and rewarding. It allows the instructor and pupil to learn a skill without the challenge of a jump. To start off we need to have some mastery of the canter on a straight line. Then an understanding of change of lead over a fence or pole. Lastly, the ability to adjust the length of the canter stride. Lots to work on. Initially, as always, make it simple.

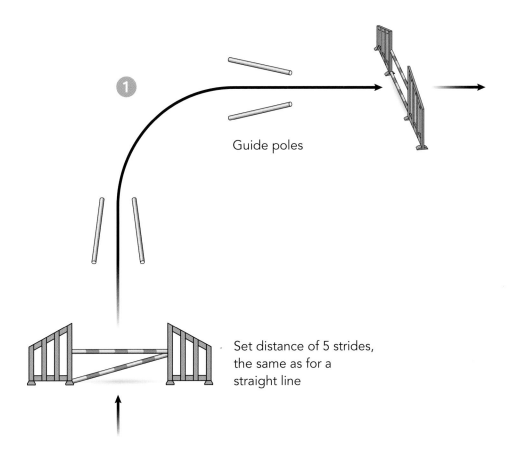

Guide poles

Set distance of 5 strides, the same as for a straight line

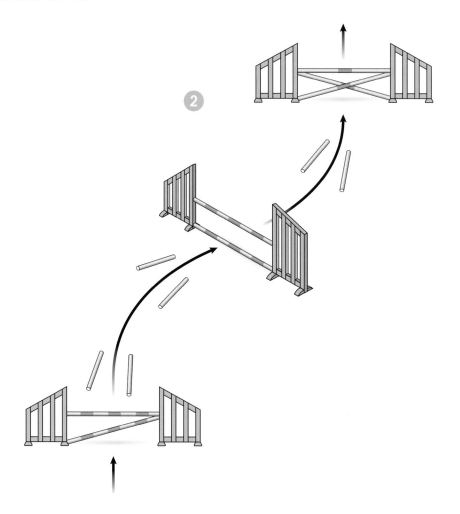

- practise an approach off each rein

- change the direction

- guide rails take you to the centre of jump at 90 degrees

- encourage regularity of stride

- lengthen or shorten to make it fit

- practise the aid for 'following the lead rein'.

Develop the exercise by introducing corners, arrowheads and skinnies into the line. One is likely to be in more control at the first jump, therefore start off with this being a simple corner or arrowhead or skinny.

The rider is often very focused on this first element and forgets to ride the canter between element one and two. As the partnership becomes more skilful so the degree of difficulty increases. One could end up with something like this for a more advanced horse.

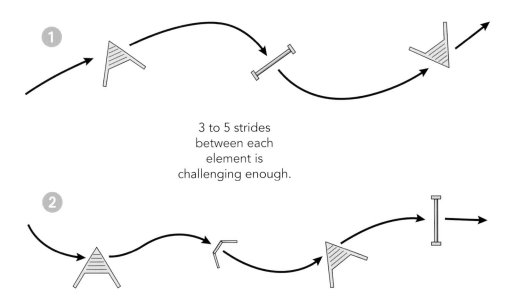

3 to 5 strides between each element is challenging enough.

Both of these exercises have their challenges:

- drifting in and out of the chosen line
- drifting off the true line at corners
- finding the right canter for the question
- being adjustable between the questions.

Do not try these too soon. To say you've jumped the difficult ones doesn't mean it has been a good experience. Take your time and … make it look easy!

10

The Course Walk

Walking the course is a key part of the competition. Done well it can improve the likelihood of a good result. There are, however, many pitfalls. It has a number of functions:

- To find out the route the course takes.

- To study the jumps and the questions they ask.

- To relate the questions to the horse being ridden.

- To understand the ground conditions.

- To measure the course.

- To memorise the time markers.

The age and experience of the rider and horse will dictate how much information is required. Too much information can be as much of a problem as too little. Inappropriate information can effect judgement. Let's deal with the ideal scenario first.

The Instructor-Pupil Walk

The instructor must know the pupil and horse. Know their capabilities, strengths and weaknesses. Understand the pupil as an individual and how they take in and use information. They will have seen this in training and hence develop a relationship. Most if not all the issues that will be met on the cross-country course should have been practised, which improves the confidence of the rider.

It is vital that the instructor does not try to teach more information than already practised in training. The instructor must also not try and impress the pupil with their own knowledge. The instructor must know how much information the pupil is able to assimilate, as in the 'heat of competition', time 'thinking' can create indecision. Often a perfectly good result can come from no information but a clear direction of 'jump here'! This leaves no room for indecision on the part of the rider. Instructor knowledge of the horse's habits is also crucial. It enables him to help the pupil to walk and then ride the correct line, taking all the necessary precautions to correct the horse's bad habits.

In this instance there is a balance to be struck. By talking about the horse's problems one is also alerting the rider to their likely occurence. Here the instructor's discretion is required. I think the pupil *should* know, just don't dwell on the subject. It is very helpful to remind the pupil of the way they jumped this kind of jump in training. It reinforces good thoughts and experiences.

As the courses become more complex and the pupils more educated so more information may be given. The expression 'beat the course designer' now becomes more relevant. As competitors, we pit our wits against the designer. As designers they create problems for us to solve. It is the trainer's responsibility to ensure that the homework has been done and that the partnership is up to the task.

Good course designers relate jump questions. As trainers we must ensure that our pupils relate the questions still to come with the ones they have just answered. The course designer is waiting to see if the rider 'reads the question' and then understands the next question.

By analysing each jump, especially combinations, we help our pupils to make a plan to suit their horse. Not everyone should be encouraged to 'go the straight route', there may be very good reasons why the alternative route may be appropriate.

The 'what happens if…' scenario must also be looked at. This is not negative thinking but realistic and practical. All is not lost with a run out but the alternative route must have been walked and planned.

Avoid having distractions when walking the course, such as:

- A group of friends chatting!

- Other competitors – different horses and issues.

- Other trainers – different ways of saying things.

- Family – all sorts of issues!

- Switch off the mobile.

The Group Walk

Often trainers will be asked to take a group of riders on a course walk. *Beware*, both as a trainer and a rider. When the trainer knows all the pupils, it is much easier than when they don't. Not knowing the rider it is very difficult to give relevant advice. One can really only work on generalities, explaining in a very non-specific way some of the issues riders should be aware of. All too often the uncertain rider becomes more unclear of what to do when there is too much information which is not relevant to them.

The Celebrity Walk

Fun to do for a rider and coach but fraught with dangers for all:

The Celebrity…keen to impress, full of stories, lots of 'I remember'… does not know horse, rider or coach, becomes too influential.

The Coach…often in awe, keen to learn new thoughts, ideas and expressions, often knows just as much.

The Rider…starstruck, hangs on every word, takes in everything right or wrong, absorbs information which may not be relevant, begins to doubt the coach, because they hear differing views from the celebrity.

Parents and Family…too easily impressed by the personality, judgement becomes influenced. Pressure applied to rider and coach as a result.

11

The Competition

The Warm-Up

There is a need to understand and coach what to do during the warm-up at a competition. There are many issues for both horse and rider that come together at a difficult time. Unless one is aware of these they can be misunderstood and hence mishandled. Tension, excitement, anxiety to please, time pressures, ground/space difficulties, 'team pressures' etc … When preparing for a competition it is important for all that are going to be present to know what happens and what part they play. This knowledge will help the smooth running and reduce the tensions of this phase. The horse also feels the pressure. It is possible to move quietly and quickly without appearing to be in a hurry. The horse mustn't feel that the handler is in a 'flap'.

Both horses and riders will often react differently from the way they do at home. Some become more 'outward' and others 'withdraw'. Know your horse and rider.

Time, allowing the partnership to return to as near normal as is possible at a competition, is never wasted time. Allow the partnership to return to the habits of how they jump at home and avoid them trying to do something different or mimic another rider's warm-up. Keep it simple and don't get drawn into what other riders or coaches do.

The Rehabilitation

Time must be taken after a cross-country school or competition to re-habilitate. (Dictionary definition: restore to rights, restore to previous condition.) Taking one step back in the training allows the coach to rebuild if necessary or to confirm what has been learnt.

The system of peaks and troughs in training is important. The peak is the competition, the trough is the retraining or rehabilitation. Failure to do so often leads to bad habits not being corrected, confidence not being restored, a lack of awareness that there is an issue to correct.

By doing smaller and more gymnastic jumping in trot or canter after a competition allows us to 'cool the brain' after the 'heat' of competition.

12

Tack and Equipment

This subject is a book in itself. I do not intend to make it so, however, there are some important principles to remember when going cross-country and as trainers we should make sure we remember them.

- belt and braces…

- better safe than sorry…

- if it does not harm but might do good….

These are the expressions our parents used to say to which we replied 'stop fussing'. It's not fussing, it's just taking every possible precaution to mitigate the dangers. It's sensible.

Saddles

The development of a whole new concept in saddle design, in some ways, has changed the way we ride. There is no doubt that the improvement in design, materials and how horses move and perform underneath the saddle, is progress. Saddles as a fashion statement or a 'must have … make or model' is not.

For cross-country, most experts will agree on the following statements:

1. A flat seat is advisable.

2. Some knee roll is helpful.

3. Close contact is helpful.

Saddles are expensive and people don't want to keep changing them. Change only becomes necessary, apart from wear and tear, when children outgrow or change shape. The changes to balance can effect security and need to be considered.

The wearing of breastplates, breastgirths and overgirths should always be considered. For me they are a must. Correctly fitted, they provide the extra security for the saddle to remain in place. Close contact saddles, with short girths are not always suited to an overgirth but adjustments should be made to make them work in order that they can be fitted for greater security.

The Martingale

This is also a vital piece of equipment for cross-country. The two acceptable types are the running and the Irish martingale.

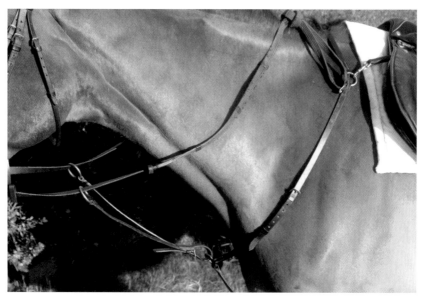

A running martingale and breastplate

Some riders believe the running martingale to be restrictive, but if fitted correctly I don't believe it to be so. However, the Irish martingale fulfils much the same function but allows much more freedom. I have always found the Irish martingale to be a useful aid to my equipment.

An Irish martingale

Leg Protection

Leg protection is advisable in all schooling and in competition. The choice of boot is endless and there are stories for and against every type ever made. Prioritise the functions and make a decision. Tendons are my priority, closely followed by the sesamoid bones. The protection of the cannon bone is the least important. Lightness and stability are vital. A material that does not hold or retain water is also important, to avoid carrying extra weight in the limbs.

Overreach Boots

Worth having, although again, one will hear stories of problems. The main problem is them inverting in mud making them redundant. There is also the story of them being caught by a hind foot when jumping out of water. I still believe they are worthwhile.

Bits and Bitting

Most riders have a preference for how much rein pressure they have when going cross-country. It is important for them to be comfortable, as this allows for the correct 'feel' of riding to a fence. Too strong a contact and they often feel they are being run away with, and too light a contact they question whether the horse is really 'there' in front of the leg.

The first and most important consideration is to bit the horse with a mouthpiece that fits and is comfortable. The horse must respond to the actions of the legs and reins to produce an adjustable pace.

There are hundreds of bits available, so which one to choose? It is impossible to advise each and every reader of a suitable bit for their horse. Here are some useful tips for choosing the right one and for what to avoid:

- use as mild a bit as you can

- make sure it fits the horse or pony (see Pony Club Manual)

- check the rules to make sure it is legal

- don't follow fashion

- don't listen to gossip or uneducated advice.

Borrow if you can before you decide to buy. Then practise to see if it gives the correct 'feel' and the correct responses from the horse. Don't just practise in the arena, go cross-country and give it more than just a few jumps. The feel should be positive (a little more than show jumping) but not pulling.

The responses must never be:

- tucking the head in on to the neck

- going above the bit

- jumping hollow

- running through the bit

- becoming one-sided

- becoming anxious.

The incorrect bit and response can produce bad riding with disastrous results.

Bit Birs

These are circular bit guards with a brush on the inside. They are very effective at straightening a horse that leans on one side of the mouth. Often this leaning can cause sore mouths or difficult handling, i.e. hard to turn or keep straight and become distracting to the real job of going cross-country. They should be introduced to the horse in a school situation to ensure understanding. It may take a few days for the horse to become comfortable.

If the horse leans on the right, fit the Bit Bir on the left. This will close against the left cheek and encourage him to be more responsive to the right rein.

Bit bir

Bit Birs are a useful addition to the tack room as a training aid but are not allowed to be used in Pony Club competitions.

Hats and Body Protectors

You only have one head! So it does make sense to have the best hat you can afford. Check it complies with the current rules and have it professionally fitted.

Too often hats are bought for the fashionable look and not for the function – of protecting your head.

Look after your hat. Don't throw it around, because each knock or bang it receives can reduce its effectiveness. If you have had a fall and there is a hint of the hat having received a knock, seek professional advice. You will probably be advised to buy a new one. Don't grumble.

Body protectors must be comfortable and of an approved safety standard. Much research has gone into their design over recent years. Check what the professionals use and again seek advice. Fashion is not a priority... safety is.

Studs

A topic that produces much discussion.

The use of studs is undoubtedly influenced by the many 'if only...' stories: competitions lost through not having studs, the right studs, enough studs or studs in the correct place. There are also views voiced of some of the dangers to horse and rider.

On balance I believe they are worth using. It is difficult to quantify their value, or to decide in which phase their greater value lies. So much depends on the ground conditions and the difficulty of the questions to be asked and the balance of the partnership.

Horses do need to get used to wearing them. It changes the sliding action of their feet especially in trot. Some horses find this off-putting. Logic would dictate that two studs in each shoe, one on either heel, would be more symmetrical for the horse and its action. There is, however, a view that the inside stud can cause brushing injuries.

My view is that I am happy to run with just an outside stud in as I do not think the asymmetry is significant. I am also happy to have two in. However, I always make sure the inside stud is smaller and round to avoid any likely injury.

Hard ground with short grass is often the most difficult for horses to retain their balance, especially when doing dressage and show jumping.

Opposite are some pictures of shoes with a variety of studs. As you will see none them are 'fancy' but they function very well.

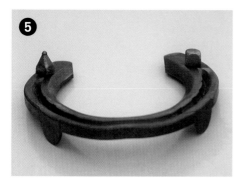

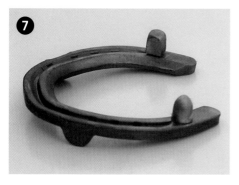

1. Normal ground
2. Soft ground
3. and 4. Muddy ground
5. and 6. Hard ground
7. Heavy ground

107

13

Conclusion

The mnemonic K.I.S.S., **Keep It Stunningly Simple** is very appropriate for cross-country riding. To enable us to keep it simple we must have certain skills in place. Sometimes learning these skills can be challenging but once learnt they open the door to some exhilarating experiences cross country.

Watching the top competitors in any sport become unconsciously competent, performing with ease, using skills which look so natural, is such a pleasure for us all. It must surely be our aim as coaches and instructors to teach these skills in order that the children of the Pony Club can develop a sound foundation of safe, competitive cross-country riding. This foundation will allow us to build and develop the next generation of riders who enjoy their sport yet are competitive and safe.

Enjoy yourself…

Index